Construction SITE

FORKLIFTS

Dan Osier

New York

Published in 2014 by The Rosen Publishing Group, Inc.
29 East 21st Street, New York, NY 10010

First Edition

Editor: Amelie von Zumbusch
Book Design: Andrew Povolny
Photo Research: Katie Stryker

Photo Credits: Cover, p. 15 iStockphoto/Thinkstock; p. 5 Thomas Barwick/Stone/Getty Images; p. 7 ekipaj/Shutterstock.com; p. 9 Rich Legg/E+/Getty Images; p. 11 Sorbis/Shutterstock.com; p. 13 Lloyd Paulson/Shutterstock.com; p. 17 nikshor/Shutterstock.com; p. 19 ndoeljindoel/Shutterstock.com; p. 21 George Doyle/Stockbyte/Thinkstock; p. 23 Michael Westhoff/E+/Getty Images.

Library of Congress Cataloging-in-Publication Data

Osier, Dan, author.
Forklifts / by Dan Osier. — First edition.
pages cm. — (Construction site)
Includes index.
ISBN 978-1-4777-3245-8 (library) — ISBN 978-1-4777-2956-4 (pbk.) —
ISBN 978-1-4777-3033-1 (6-pack)
1. Forklift trucks—Juvenile literature. 2. Construction equipment—Juvenile literature. I. Title. II. Title: Fork lifts.
TL296.O85 2014
621.8′63—dc23

2013022416

Manufactured in the United States of America

CPSIA Compliance Information:W14PK3 For Further Information contact Rosen Publishing, New York, New York at 1-800-237-9932

Contents

Forklifts are cool! They can lift big loads.

You can see them at
building sites.

You can see them in warehouses, too.

Some forklifts have **counterweights** at the back. These help them not tip over.

Telescopic forklifts have **booms**. Their booms can stretch out. This lets them lift loads very high.

A B C D E F G H I

The biggest forklift companies are in Japan, Germany, and the United States.

MAX CAP

The Yale company made the first forklift trucks.

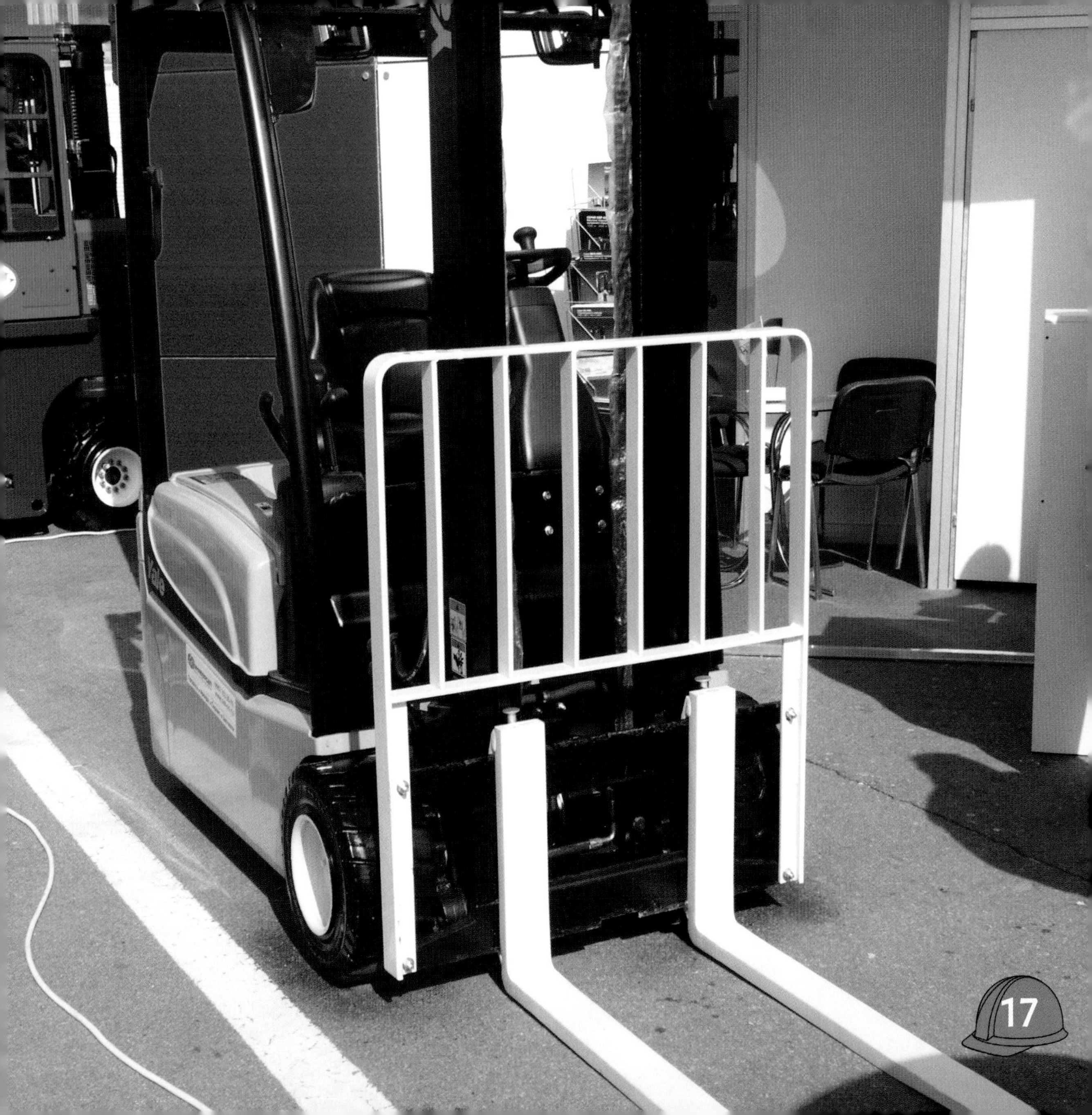

It takes skill to drive a forklift.

You also must be at least 18 years old.

Would you like to drive a forklift when you grow up?

HOW AM I DRIVING?

WORDS TO KNOW

boom

counterweight

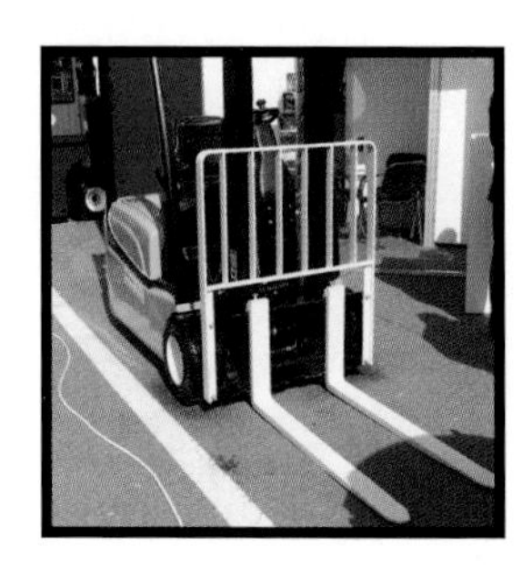

forklift

WEBSITES

Due to the changing nature of Internet links, PowerKids Press has developed an online list of websites related to the subject of this book. This site is updated regularly. Please use this link to access the list:
www.powerkidslinks.com/cs/forkli/

INDEX